The FATHER Provides

By KATHIE JOHNSON WRIGHT

Abraham took his only son, Isaac, to that place God directed, so that he might offer his son to God. When Abraham arrived on the mountain to offer up Isaac as a sacrifice, Isaac asked his father, "Where is the lamb for the sacrifice?" **His father responded, "God will provide."**

Excerpt based on Genesis 22:1-8 (NIV)

Trilogy Christian Publishers

A Wholly Owned Subsidiary of Trinity Broadcasting Network

2442 Michelle Drive

Tustin, CA 92780

For information, address Trilogy Christian Publishing

Rights Department, 2442 Michelle Drive, Tustin, Ca 92780.

Trilogy Christian Publishing/ TBN and colophon are trademarks of Trinity Broadcasting Network.

For information about special discounts for bulk purchases, please contact Trilogy Christian Publishing.

Manufactured in the United States of America

10 9 8 7 6 5 4 3 2 1

Library of Congress Cataloging-in-Publication Data is available.

ISBN: 978-1-63769-748-1

E-ISBN: 978-1-63769-749-8

Dedication

This book is dedicated to all fathers who work so diligently to make a difference in the lives of their children. Specifically, I dedicate this book to my dad, Reginald Whipple, Sr.

Preface

These pages contain some of the experiences I had with my own father. This book is written to honor fathers everywhere. It is important to share the significance of fatherhood because the role of the father is being systematically attacked and destroyed in our culture. The role of the father has been devalued extensively. Hopefully, someone reading this book will remember his or her father, and honor our Heavenly Father.

Acknowledgement

I acknowledge some very special people in my life who have been my inspiration in bringing this book together.

Without my mother, Mary Lizzie Whipple, I do not believe I would be the woman I am today. She is my greatest inspiration in life. I thank God for my parents and eleven siblings: Reginald, Mary Ann, Ernest, Jannett, Steven, Milton, Pamela, Vince, Angelette, Ronald and Rita. They have all shaped my life in some form or fashion. As a result, I am able to reflect and write this book.

My special thanks to my spouse, John Wallace Wright, who allows me all the liberties I need to write, to meditate, to pray and live life to its fullest. My dear husband, you are a Godsend.

I acknowledge my son, Terence Shelton Johnson, who is the joy of my life and a wonderful, delightful young man. You are the reflection of your deceased father, Terence Wendell Johnson, who laid the groundwork for you as the pleasant, God-fearing young man you are.

I thank God for special friends in my life. Because of their influence, I have been encouraged and pushed to write and preach. Thank you, Griffin Lotson. You have encouraged me to be the maverick you are. You said write it. So, here it is.

A very special thank you to those who have stood by me in ministry, especially when the going got rough: Essie Ball, Mary Alice Liggens, Juanester Hunter and Chinester Graves.

Table of Contents

Introduction

> ***Children, obey your parents in the Lord, for this is right. "Honor your father and mother"—which is the first commandment with a promise— "so that it may go well with you and that you may enjoy long life on the earth." Fathers, do not exasperate your children; instead, bring them up in the training and instruction of the Lord.***
>
> Ephesians 6:1-4 (NIV)

During the month of February, we celebrate my dad's birthday. These pages contain some of the experiences I had with my own father. This book is written to honor fathers everywhere as America is rapidly becoming a fatherless society, or perhaps more accurately, an absentee father society. The importance and influence of fathers in families has been in significant decline. We need fathers to step up and take their rightful places in the family. The Lord encourages fathers and admonishes fathers to train and instruct. It is my hope that someone reading this book will remember his or her father, and honor our heavenly Father.

Prologue

Your life is changing. You may be on the threshold of new beginnings. Perhaps you are about to enter that binding relationship. Perhaps the baby is due soon. You have so many questions. Will I make a good parent? Can we survive having children? How do I care for my children? What is my role as father?

Just know that you are not alone. These are lifelong questions as we journey through time. We want to make the rights choices and the best decisions regarding life, marriage, children and our loved ones.

There are plenty of reasons why it can be difficult for some men to push ahead into parenthood. Maybe your relationship with your dad was not a model of emotions, vulnerability and meaningful conversations. But you do know, you want to be a Godly father.

Let's consider three primary characteristics that men, if they are to be men of God, need to have as part of their character. **The Father: Provides, Instructs, and Protects.**

The Father PROVIDES

Together, my parents raised twelve children: six boys and six girls. I remember growing up in rural Georgia; we did not get everything we wanted, but we never went hungry. My mother was a homemaker and Dad always worked. We were not wealthy by any means. But I do not remember a time we did not have clothes on our backs and a roof over our heads.

> ***"Therefore take no thought, saying, 'What shall we eat?' or, 'What shall we drink?' or, 'Wherewithal shall we be clothed?' for your heavenly Father knoweth that ye have need of all these things"*** (Matthew 6:31-32 KJV).

During the last forty years of his employment, Daddy worked at the kaolin plant in the Middle Georgia area. He worked in the plant as a calciner operator. I never fully understood what he did, nor knew his wages, but this job provided for his family.

I can vaguely remember all those years ago, when he purchased our first home. I must have been about three years old. It was a two-bedroom, white, wood house. But as the family grew, Daddy added on another bedroom to separate the boys from the girls.

He often returned home after a day's work, tired but ready to put his sons to work. Daddy was self-enterprising. To provide for his family, he learned to fix everything from sheetrock to adding another room. I do not know from where he acquired his skills, but Daddy fixed or worked on everything. He learned to fix appliances and leaky faucets, work on cars, and cut grass. He, in turn, passed these skills on to his boys.

> ***"But my God shall supply all your need according to his riches in glory..."*** (Philippians 4:19 KJV).

Not only did he fix household appliances, the housing infrastructure and structure, but Daddy could cook. When mom was off to the hospital having another young one, my dad would cook. The downside to Dad's cooking was that he made you eat everything on your plate. It wasn't that the food he cooked for us wasn't good, it was the amount of food he put on your plate! He expected his children to eat every morsel. I did not stomach this well. I learned to slip my portion of food to my brother. He was pleased to consume every bit of it.

> ***"Consider the ravens: for they neither sow nor reap; which neither have storehouse nor barn; and God feedeth them: how much more are ye better than the fowls?"*** (Luke 12:24 KJV).

Although my mom would frequent the local Piggly Wiggly for groceries, we had a smokehouse my dad built and a large garden which he planted. Every year, a hog was slaughtered so we had plenty of meats. We not only harvested our own vegetables, but he also attempted to put us to work picking other folks' peas. The freezer was always full of peas, beans, greens, squash, and corn. All that Mama did not freeze, she canned or preserved: peaches, apples, pears, pickles, and peppers. We enjoyed tomatoes, okra, radish, cucumbers, melons, Irish and sweet potatoes, sugar cane, and everything fresh from the garden.

Dad cut his sons' hair. He was sought out by others for his haircutting abilities, but Mom knew how to put certain of his efforts to an end, as she did not allow other females to bring their boys to get their haircuts. He certainly was not permitted to cut other women's hair. This also curtailed his singing attempts with his cousins who formed a quartet back in the day. Yes, Daddy could make and hold onto a dollar.

In today's terminology, my Dad always had a hustle. Whereas he was not driven by greed, he was driven to provide. He cared for and made provisions for his family.

When we needed food or clothes, Daddy provided. Outside of his regular employment, he, along with his sons, self-contracted to mow lawns, fix lawn mowers, and work on

> ***"If ye then, being evil, know how to give good gifts unto your children, how much more shall your Father which is in heaven give good things to them that ask him?"*** (Matthew 7:11 KJV).

vehicles. When the holidays rolled around, Daddy provided the family with nuts, candies, and fruit for the festive occasions and gifts and new toys at Christmastime.

If my earthly father knew how to give good gifts to his family, how much more will your heavenly Father provide and give good gifts to his children who ask. The Father wants to bless you. He is a rewarder to those who diligently seek Him.

Reflections:

My natural father provided…

My heavenly Father provides…

In my role as father, I will trust God to help me provide…

____

____

____

____

____

____

The Father GUIDES/INSTRUCTS

Now provisions, or being able to provide, go hand in hand with the next characteristic: Instruction and Guidance. Yes, my father provided or made provisions for us, but these provisions came with a strong hand of discipline.

What I remember mainly about my dad's instructions was that what was good for the boys—was good for the girls also. Daddy spelled out the "Rule of Three." You had three choices after high school. You could get a job, join the military, or get married. I chose *college*.

> ***"Fathers, do not provoke your children to anger, but bring them up in the discipline and instruction of the Lord"*** (Ephesians 6:4 RSV).

My dad made it to the eighth grade. During those times, formal education ended with the eighth grade. Afterwards, you were expected to work in the fields or help out on the farm. Daddy was proud of his education and initially thought that if eighth grade was good enough for him, then college was not necessary. Of course, by the 1970's, education for most children continued through twelfth grade.

Let me interject a few things about my mother. Mom

> ***"Hear, my son, your father's instruction, and reject not your mother's teaching"*** (Proverbs 1:8 RSV).

completed eighth grade as well. She and my dad both were the youngest children from each of their families. Mom went to school and completed school as she saw fit. In other words, if she did not want to attend school, she did not. Finally, after skipping out of school for a while, she realized it was self-defeating. She placed herself in the grade in which she thought she should have been and completed eighth grade.

When she married my dad in 1954, she had observed a few things in life. Based on her observations, she stood on the Word of God, and declared blessings over the life of her family. Now she did not know anything about a "name it and claim it" theology. But within herself, she knew there was power in her words as scripture has said, "Life and death are in the power of the tongue" (Proverbs 18:21a, HCSB). Within herself, and through the power of God, she spoke and declared blessings over her life, the life of her husband, and the life of her children. She firmly declared, "All my children will complete high school. My children will be raised in church. My children will not intermingle with relatives." With buy-in from my dad, they were on their

> ***"Train up a child in the way he should go; even when he is old he will not depart from it"*** (Proverbs 22:6 RSV).

way to rearing their offspring. They both left their lifelong Baptist roots and joined the Church of God in Christ.

So, I remember always being in church. My mom would threaten to leave us at home if we made her late one more time. Though we tried her patience, that promise was never fulfilled. My dad never threatened. He simply spoke it, and we would be in the car waiting for him.

> ***"He who spares the rod hates his son, but he who loves him is diligent to discipline him"*** (Proverbs 13:24 RSV).

My parents made frequent trips to Florida to visit his sister and her family. Mainly, it was my brother and I (we were the youngest at the time) travelling with our parents to Florida. I loved standing on the rear hump in front of the rear seat, so I could watch my daddy drive. He would provide the instructions of the road and explain road courtesy and hazards. As we travelled over 330 miles of highway, I would eventually fall asleep and awaken as we approached my aunt's home. It was during these trips that I learned to map out directions and later successfully plan my routes.

Not only did he teach us the courtesy of the road, but he also taught us good citizenship. We could not litter. Find a receptacle, and properly dispose of trash. If you see paper on the ground, pick it up. So, it is hard even today, to just walk by paper on the ground and not pick it up. One, definitely, was not allowed to throw trash out of the car window. These disciplines follow you through life.

Daddy was a strong disciplinarian. Over the progression of time, I would hear the instructions given to my two older sisters and two older brothers. I would latch on to every word because I always wanted to please my daddy, and thus avoid the wrath that followed if I did not.

> ***"My son, do not despise the Lord's discipline or be weary of his reproof, for the Lord reproves him whom he loves, as a father the son in whom he delights"*** (Proverbs 3:11-12 RSV).

Daddy imposed a curfew twelve o'clock midnight for his sons and daughters. No smoking, alcohol consumption, cussing, and no secular music was allowed. We must attend Sunday School every Sunday and worship services every first and third Sundays. At that time, worship opportunities were not every Sunday since the pastor was only available on two Sundays. Our stoic little family always shared meals together. We dare not begin eating our food until the grace was said and each of us recited scripture.

I remember during my college years, my freshman year in particular, my dorm mates liked to roam the streets at night. They coaxed me out of my room one night, as they declared that they were tired of my "going to bed with the chickens." Reluctantly, I travelled with them that night from Milledgeville to Macon. There were about five of us. The vehicle broke down in Macon. The car was pushed off the street, over in front of the liquor store. Another dorm mate and I were told to wait with the car. My dorm mate feared that the police would come by and question us about being in front of the liquor store after midnight. While she was looking out for the police, I was praying and looking out for my daddy's car. I prayed because I knew if my dad saw me out that time of night and in front of a liquor store, I might not make it back to college life.

Start children off on the way they should go, and even when they are old, they will not turn from it. We grew up with provisions and the guidance of my parents. We safely returned to campus. However, I did not venture off campus again with these young ladies.

Reflections:

My natural father instructed…

____

____

____

____

____

____

The instructions of my heavenly Father are given…

____

____

____

____

____

____

As a father to my children, I will teach them…

____

____

____

____

____

____

The Father PROTECTS

God sees what we don't see.

As a youngster, we often think we know most things. What father doesn't protect their child even when their child doesn't know any better? God protects us when we try to do our own thing. God can see what we cannot see.

"Trust in the Lord with all your heart and lean not on your own understanding; in all your ways submit to him, and he will make your paths straight" (Proverbs 3:5-6 NIV).

For example, let us picture a baby on a bed who is constantly trying to get over the edge of the bed. The baby cannot see, but his father can see. He can hurt himself if he falls off, so his father blocks him from falling off. Sometimes we get disappointed when things do not go our way, and wonder, God why don't you open this door? Why didn't that relationship last? Why did this happen to me?

"You, Lord, will keep the needy safe and will protect us forever from the wicked" (Psalm 12:7 NIV).

God sees what we cannot see, and He is going to protect us whether we like it or not. If only you knew. Sometimes we ask for things that will end up harming us if God answered.

Sometimes He allows relationships to end that are going to be harmful to us, and closes doors that will end up detrimental for us. God is faithful! We must trust that He knows what He is doing.

My dad could see what I could not see when I planned a trip to New Jersey. During my junior year of college, Dad bought me a car. It was a hooptie, but it was the best he could afford. During my externship in Albany, Georgia, I needed a vehicle. So, he got me a car. Daddy instructed the car was to serve my externship.

> ***"What feels like rejection is often God's protection when you're heading in the wrong direction."***
> –Donna Partow

While in Albany, I befriended many because I had a car. One of my college friends and I decided we would drive the car to her home state, New Jersey. Against my dad's advice, we drove the car to New Jersey. Of course, as Dad predicted, the vehicle broke down… in several states. After fifteen hours of driving straight through, (including our numerous stops to let the engine cool) we arrived in Philadelphia, Pennsylvania. At this point, my girlfriend realized that she did not know how to get to New Jersey because it had been ten years since she had been home. In the wee hours of the morning, I could not accept that we were lost. Instead, I fell back on the guidance of my father as I sought out a map, and routed the remainder of our trip as I should have in the beginning.

After several days, because I must prepare for my return to college, it was time to return to Georgia. Alas, the next morning, she discovered the vehicle had been stolen from where it was parked on the street! After threatening my friend that she had better not return to Georgia without my car, I had to catch the Greyhound bus back home. She had said it was okay to park the car on the street in front of her mother's home. I was disheartened, and I did not look forward to my dad's queries about the car. Upon my return, and when asked about the car, I informed them that I had chosen to catch the bus because my girlfriend needed a little more time to get back, but she would be driving it back soon. The Lord answers prayer, because she and her brothers found the car just as it was being dismantled at a chop shop. The vehicle was recovered, fixed, and she drove it back to Georgia.

Earlier in my life, I had witnessed the protection of my father. On one occasion, the police came to our home looking for one of my brothers. It was a Sunday morning, as we prepared for breakfast before going to church. My dad listened as the officer spoke. Then he called my brother outside. I remember Daddy saying to the officer, "I know where my son was, but we will let him speak."

I remember my dad being so incensed that the officer

even approached him and accused one of his sons over the words of a known drunk (as my dad phrased it). As my dad dismissed my brother, the next words I recall my dad commanding were, "Officer, you have five minutes to get off my property!" We never heard anything more concerning this matter.

Because Dad exemplified these traits, provider, instructor and protector, I trusted him. I believed that he would provide for me, that he would give me good instructions, and that he would protect me.

> ***"God is our refuge and strength, an ever-present help in trouble"*** (Psalm 46:1 NIV).

In my early teenage years, I was working. There was an incident that happened. I served as the monitor on the shuttle, where after school, we took these special needs children home in a shuttle or van provided by the development center. This was an unusual request, as I did not normally perform such a duty. I had been asked by the director to accompany the shuttle driver on his route. A few of them lived on unpaved roads in the area. As we made the final drop off, the driver took a different route that day. The driver backed the shuttle into a deserted area. Something was awry. Why are we stopping, and why are we stopping in this area? I began to fight off the shuttle driver, now my aggressor. In the process of time, I knew I was no match for this man. My strength was waning quickly. In my final attempt to fight off the shuttle driver, and as I began to succumb to my aggressor, I remember saying through my tears, "I'm going to tell *my daddy*." Something about those words struck a chord. Suddenly, he let me go. The power he had over me was gone.

Because I had a personal relationship with my daddy, I felt I could cry out to him. In essence, we all have the love and should hold a personal relationship with the sovereign Creator of the universe! It should encourage us to draw near to God and expect to find mercy, compassion and help in the time of trouble. For God is not only a Father, but by far the best and kindest of all fathers. As the psalmist declared in Psalm 18:6 (NIV), "In my distress, I called to the Lord; I cried to my God for help. From his temple he heard my voice; my cry came before him, into his ears."

I do not know what relationship you have had with your father. It may have been a close relationship, a distant relationship, or none at all. But Jehovah God is a Father to the fatherless. He is with you, even when you feel He is not. He, indeed, is a very present help in the time of trouble. Seek Him. Call on Him today. He wants to provide, guide and protect you.

Reflections

My earthly father has protected me…

My heavenly Father protects me…

As a father to my children, I have protected them…

____

____

____

____

____

____

Conclusion

Even as Abraham (Father of Many Nations) declared, so we will declare:

> As Abraham feared God and sought to please Him, God saw his faithfulness. Abraham left that place of comfort provided by his earthly father, and sought to follow the leading of his heavenly Father. God provided for, instructed and protected Abraham. So, when Abraham was called upon to offer his only son, Isaac, he was obedient and ready. That's how he was able to rename that mountain, that place of sacrifice,
> **"The-Lord-Will-Provide."**

God is calling for fathers who will step out in faith. He is calling for fathers who will pass the test. Yes, the clarion call is to fathers who are obedient to Him. Then and only then, do men become true fathers and real providers. And as the heavenly Father said unto Abraham in Genesis 22:17-18 (NKJV),

"Blessing I will bless you, and multiplying I will multiply your descendants as the stars of the heaven and as the sand which *is* on the seashore; and your descendants shall possess the gate of their enemies. In your seed all the nations of the earth shall be blessed, because you have obeyed My voice."

Young man, old and seasoned man, widowed, divorced, unmarried, whatever your status may be, won't you surrender to God and allow Him to make you whole, to give your life meaning, purpose and joy. Let Him guide you today in making you the best possible father. Trust the Father and watch Him do it!

Prayer

O Heavenly Father, I praise Your name today. I honor you. I thank you for being my Father. I surrender myself to You. Take control of my life. I know it is You, Father, who has kept me, even when I did not desire to be kept and did not follow Your instructions. Yet You provided for and protected me. As I prepare for Your kingdom, Father, continue to guide me and protect me. I humble myself before You. You are the Potter; I am the clay. Make me over again day by day.

Hopefully, the reading of this book has touched your life. If you know the Spirit of God is prompting you toward change or to take on the role for which God has called you, will you speak the following prayer over your life:

Sovereign Father, let Your Will reign in my life. I ask forgiveness and I forgive. As a father, help me to model You before my children, my family and loved ones, and even in my community. Help me to be the earthly father I did not have. And let me emulate the Godly fathers You have placed on this earth in front of me. I honor Your name. Have dominion in my life. For Yours is the kingdom, and the power and the glory forever. Amen.

Afterword

It is my hope that this book will inspire you to reach out to the Father. I honor all fathers and especially thank God for my dad. I would hope that we all strive to get back to the blueprint that God designed. Then, and only then, can we have a nation under God, and a society where generations inherit the blessings of God's favor.

God bless you…Amen.

About the Author

Kathie Johnson Wright served as Senior Pastor of the New Jerusalem-Words of Praise Church (NJ-WOP) over nineteen years. She has fed and inspired sheep over 43 years since her humble beginnings in church ministry. She was licensed as an evangelist at age nineteen.

She has received extensive training in leadership and business management. K. Johnson Wright holds both a Masters (MBA) and a Bachelors (BBA) from Georgia College and State University. She is a Certified Government Financial Manager (CGFM-Retired). K. Johnson Wright is ordained. She is a leader, conference speaker and trailblazer. She spearheaded the anointed "Empowerment for Living" radio broadcast.

For her years of devoted service to the community, K. Johnson Wright received the Congressional Distinguished Service Award. She is results-driven, as she has been consistently nominated Who's Who Among American Professional and Businesswomen and selected consecutively as

Woman of the Year. Concerned about youth, she served several years as a panelist for the Gwinnett County Youth Diversion Program. She is a member and active supporter of the Autism Society of America and advocates for people with disabilities.

K. Johnson Wright has traveled extensively throughout North America, Africa, and Europe. She enjoys preaching, speaking, teaching, reading, travelling, daily walking and playing pickleball. She is from rural Georgia, where her parents and siblings reside. She is married to Dr. John W. Wright. They have three adult children: Terence Shelton, Liana, and Jacob.

CPSIA information can be obtained
at www.ICGtesting.com
Printed in the USA
BVHW091357020222
627784BV00016B/1589